soul jazz

Arranged by Brent Edstrom

contents

ISBN 978-1-4234-5916-3

HAL•LEONARD®

7777 W. BLUEMOUND RD. P.O. BOX 13819 MILWAUKEE, WI 53213

Visit Hal Leonard Online at
www.halleonard.com

BACK AT THE CHICKEN SHACK

By JIMMY SMITH

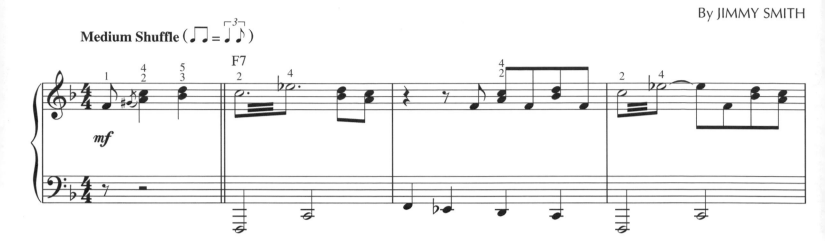

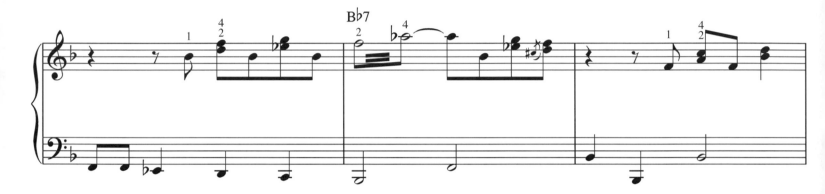

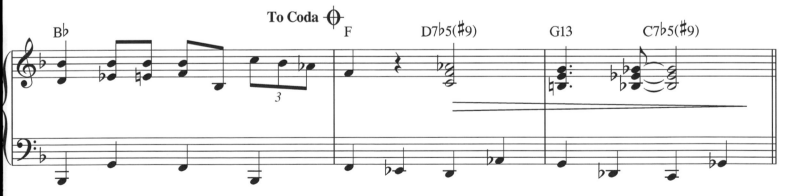

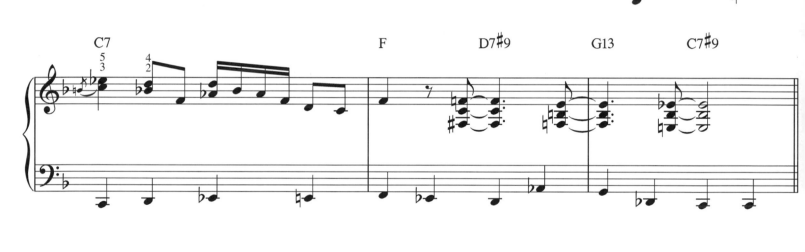

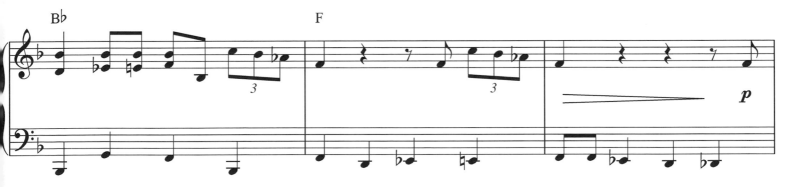

COLD DUCK TIME

By EDDIE HARRIS

Medium Rock

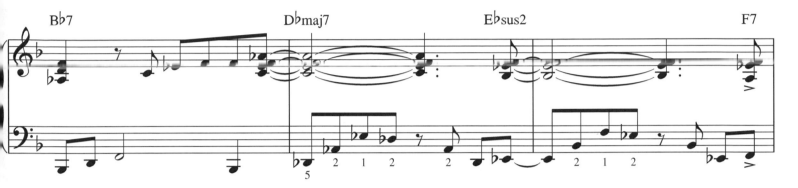

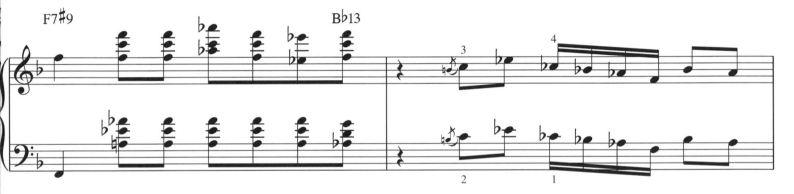

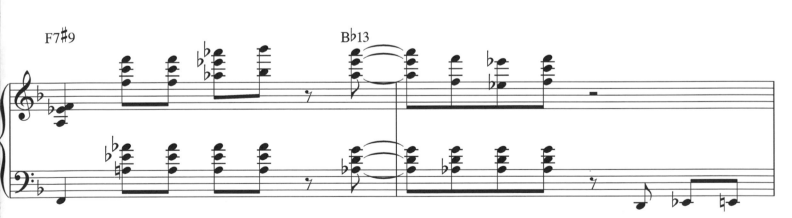

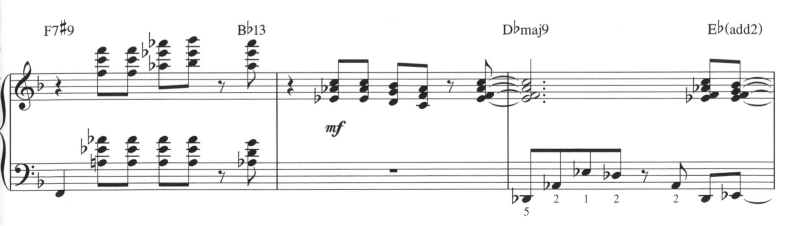

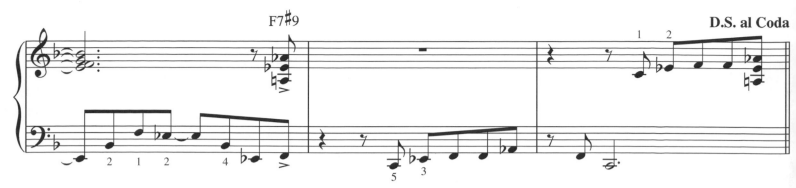

COMIN' HOME BABY

Words and Music by ROBERT DOROUGH
and BENJAMIN TUCKER

Soul Jazz

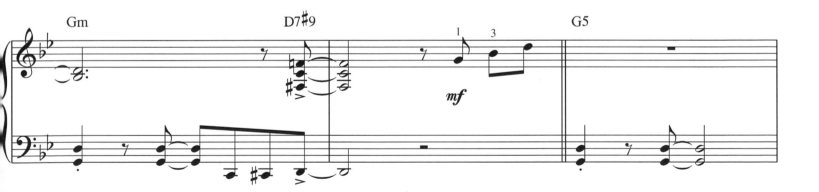

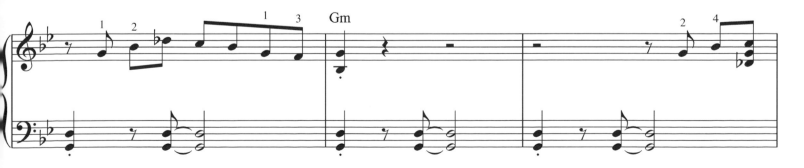

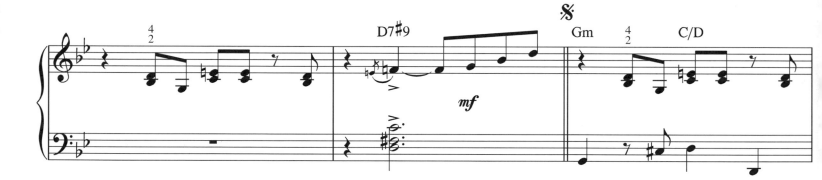

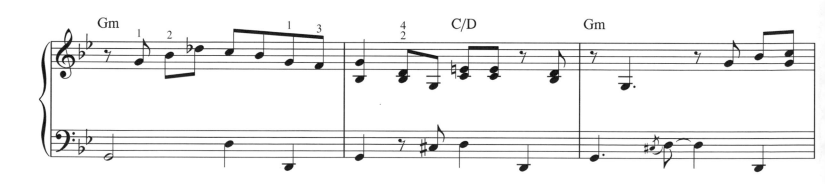

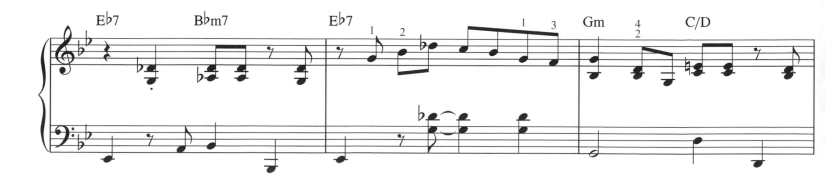

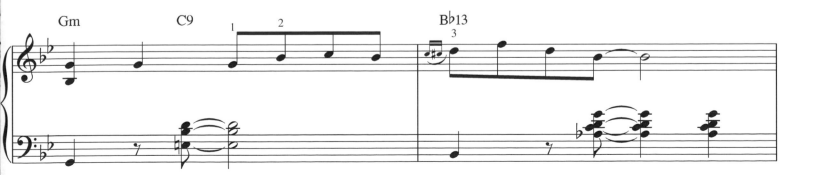

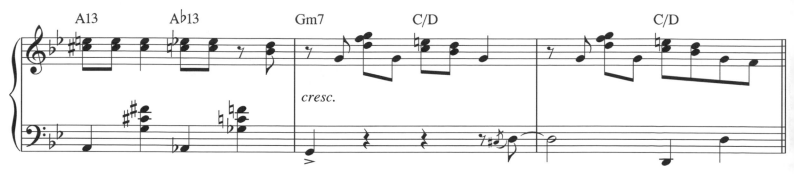

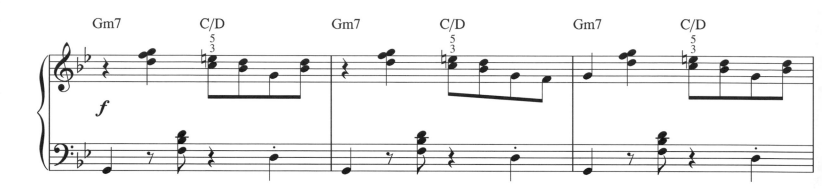

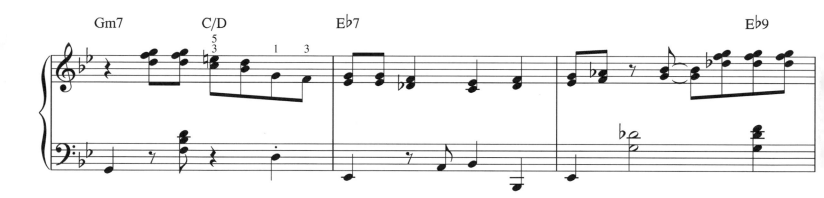

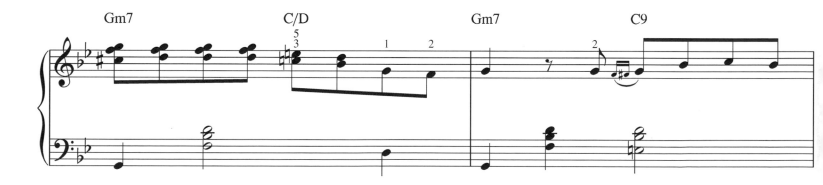

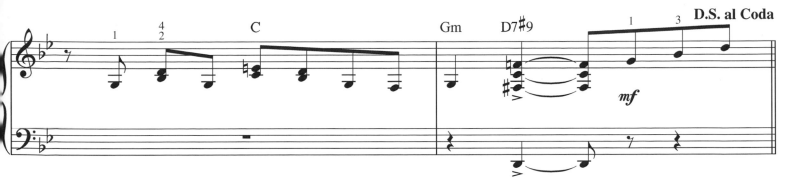

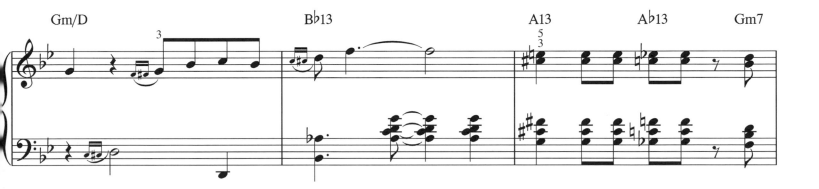

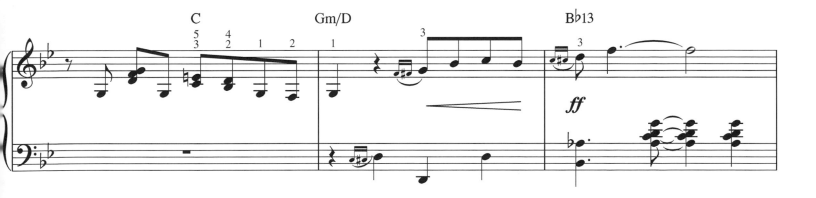

COMPARED TO WHAT

Words and Music by
EUGENE McDANIELS

Medium Gospel Rock

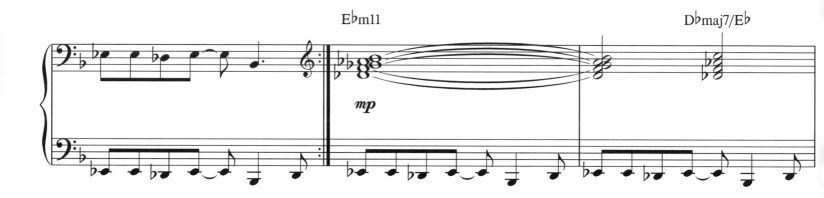

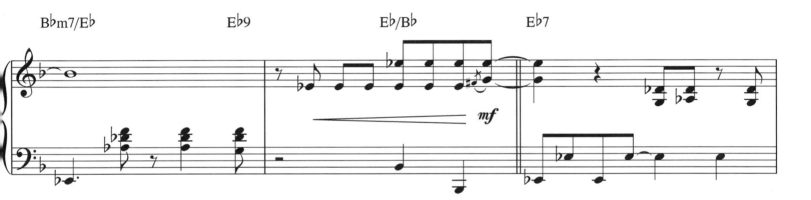

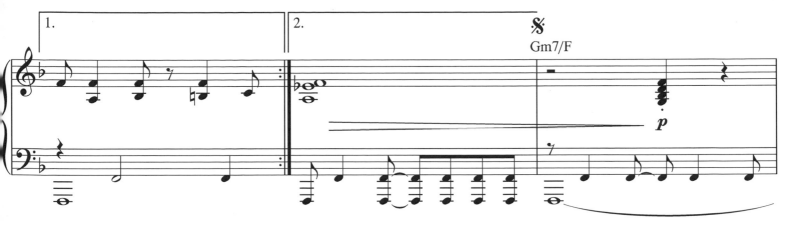

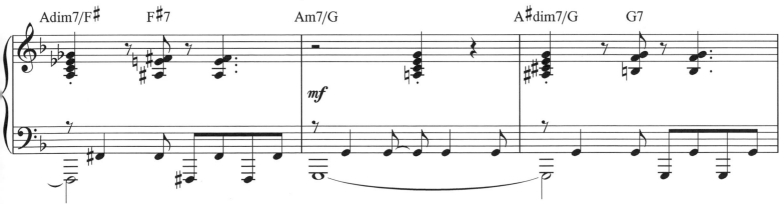

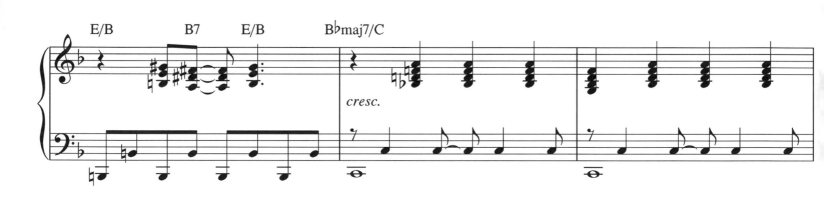

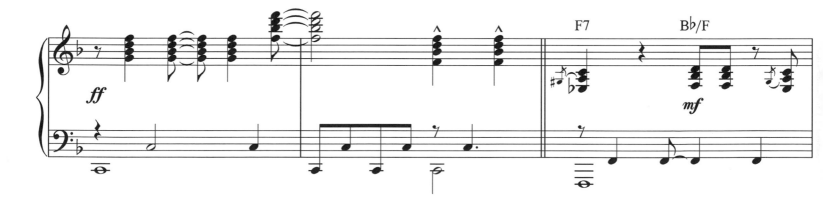

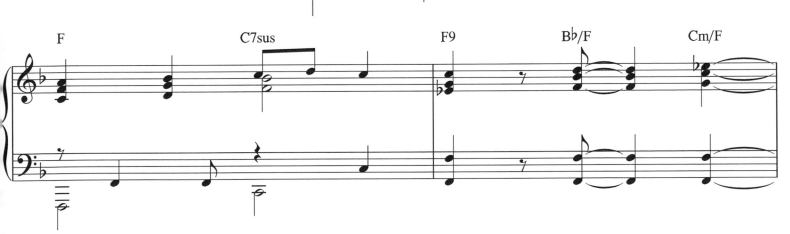

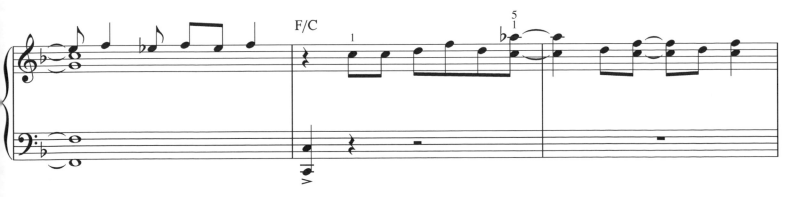

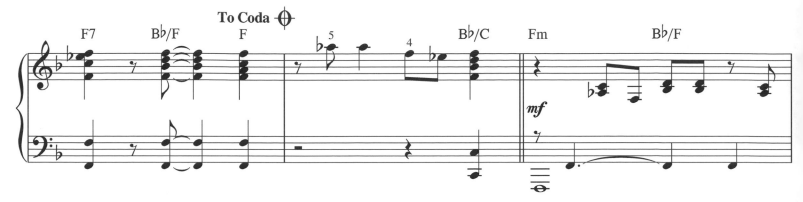

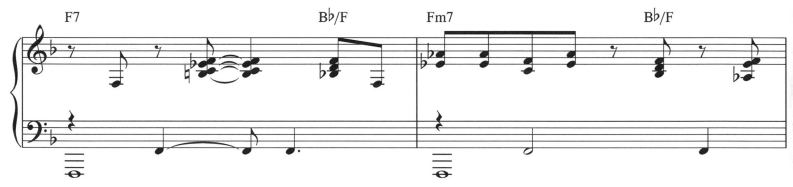

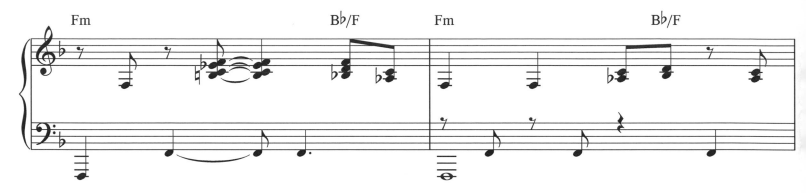

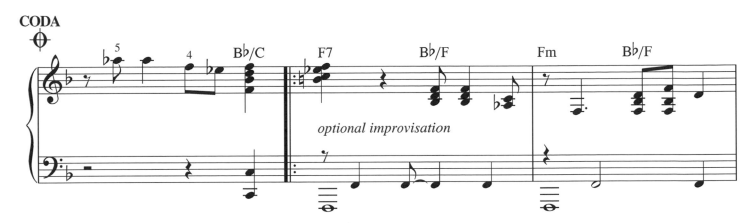

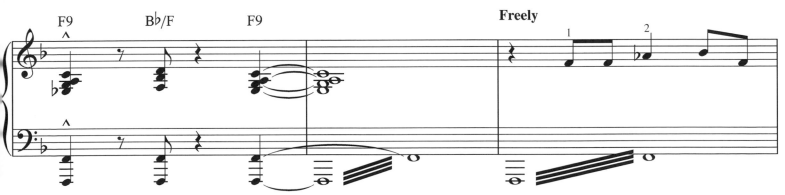

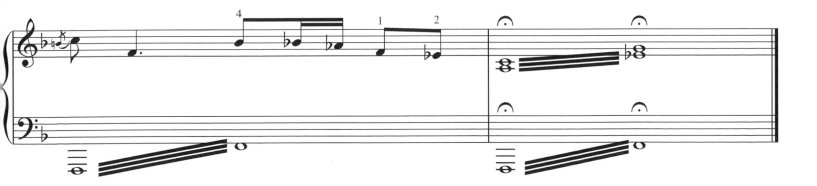

DAT DERE

By BOBBY TIMMONS

Medium Soul Jazz

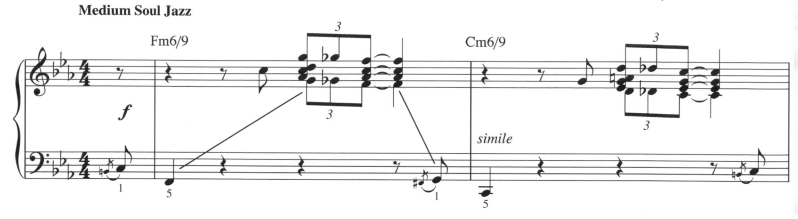

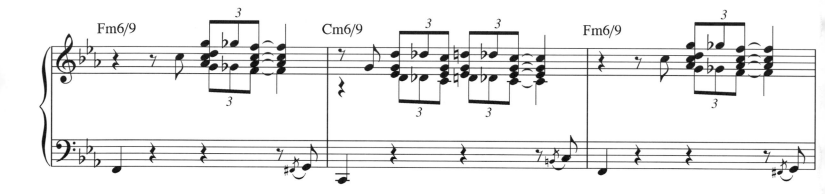

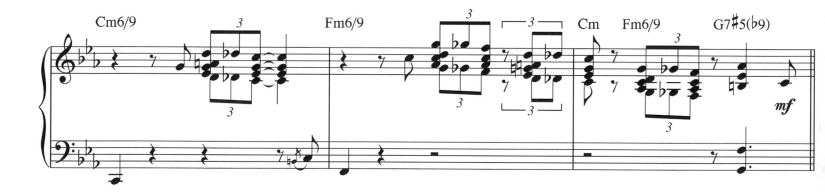

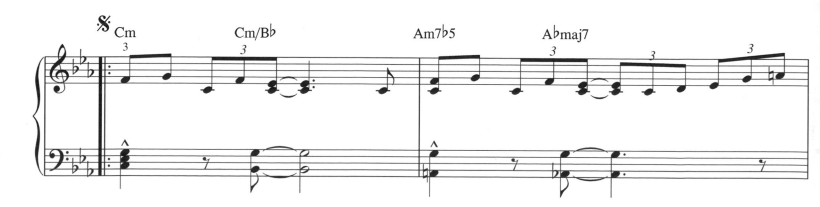

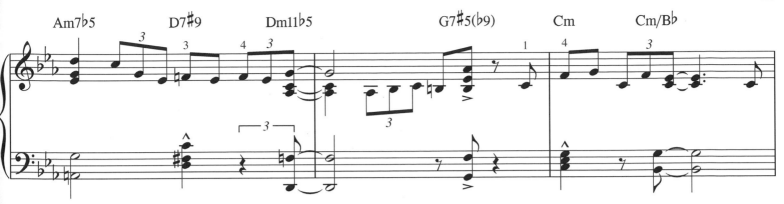

To Coda ⊕

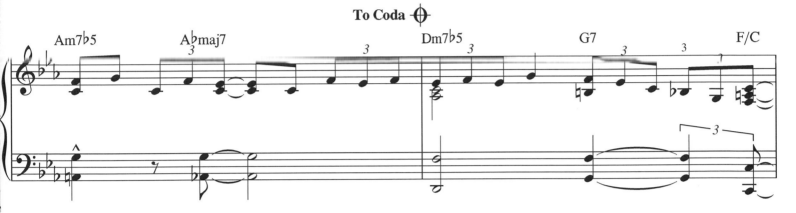

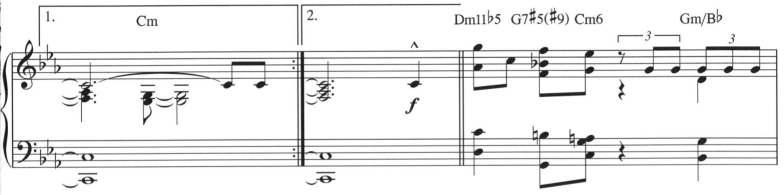

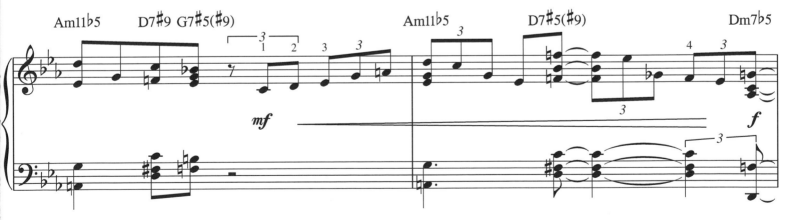

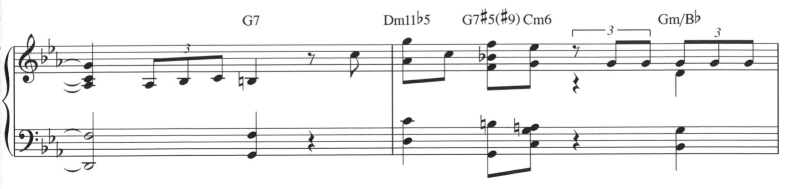

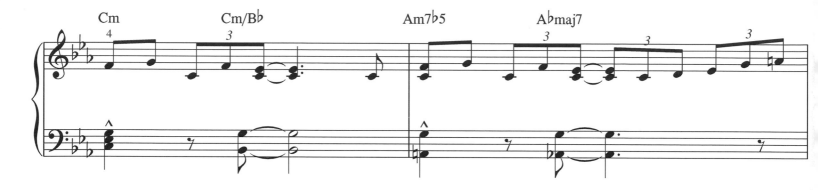

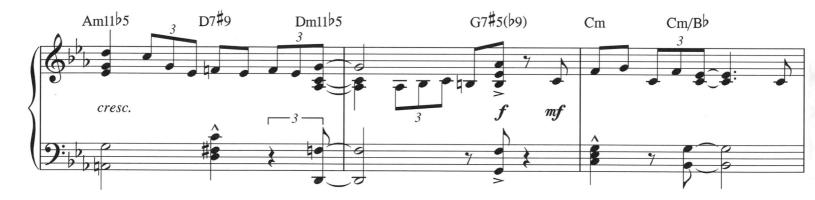

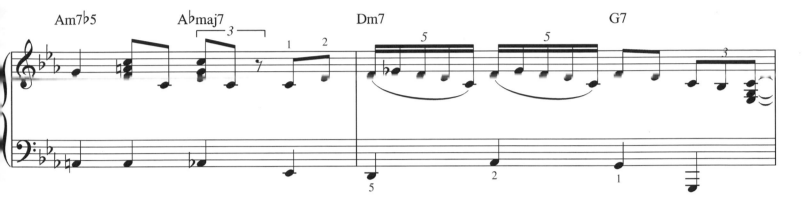

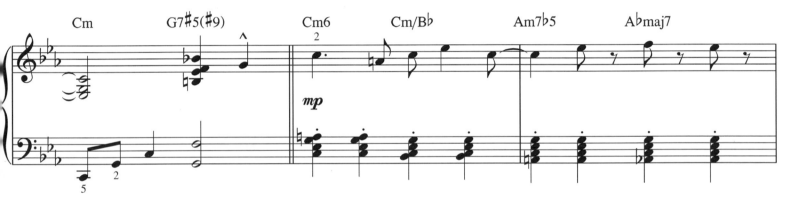

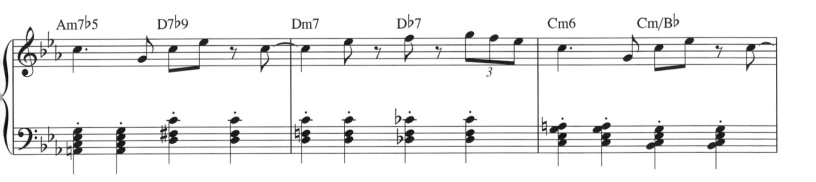

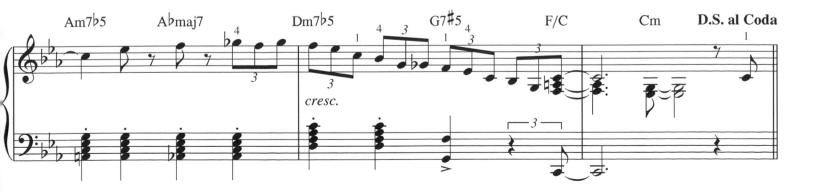

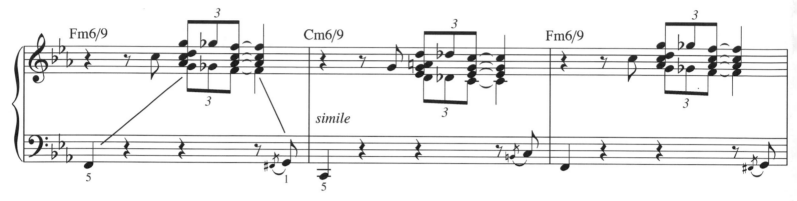

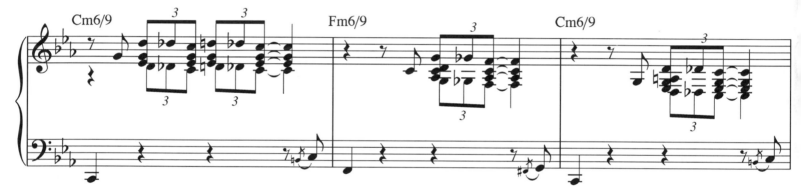

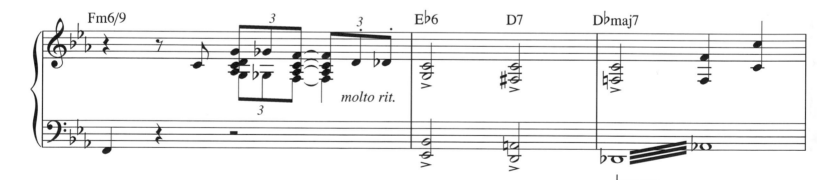

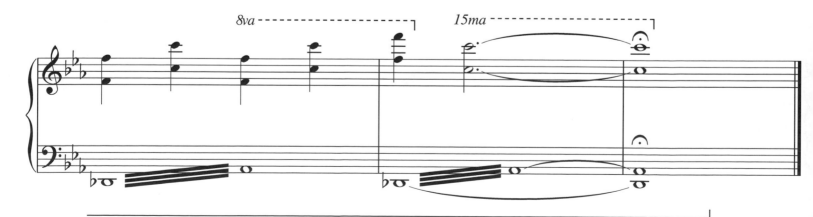

HOT TODDY

Words and Music by HERB HENDLER
and RALPH FLANAGAN

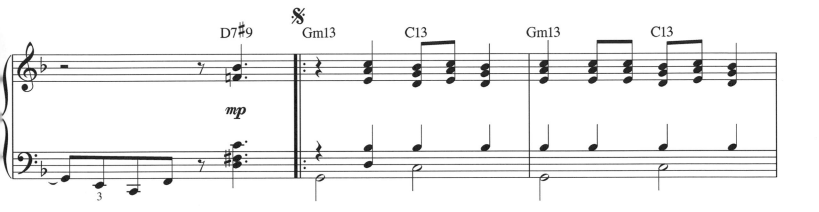

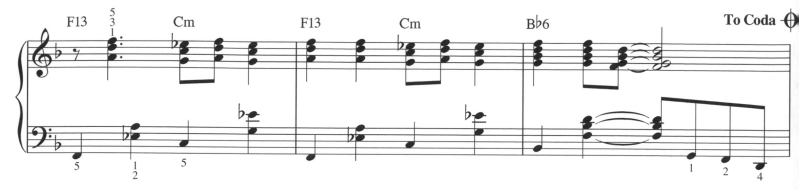

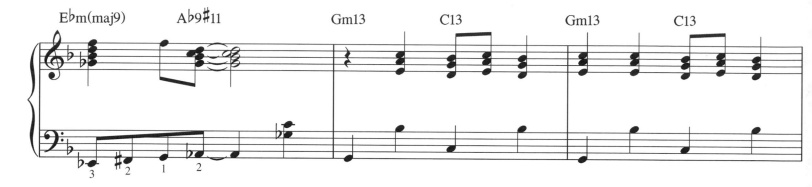

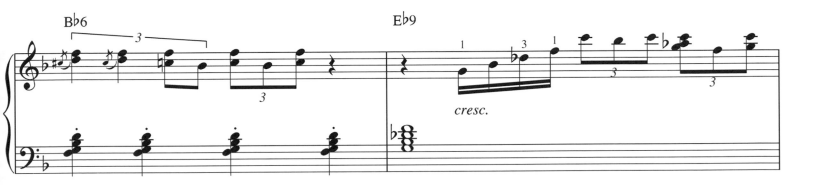

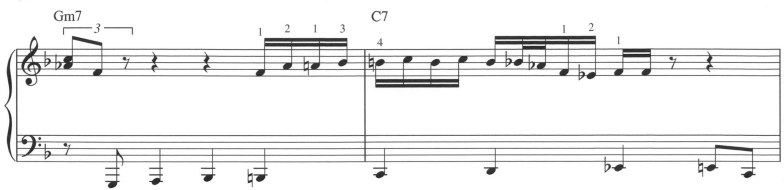

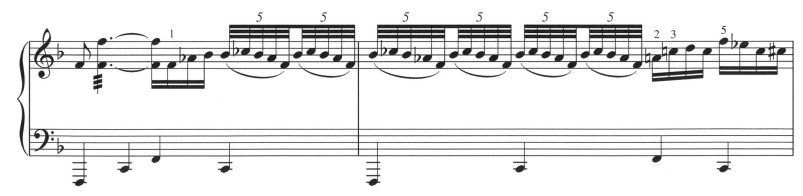

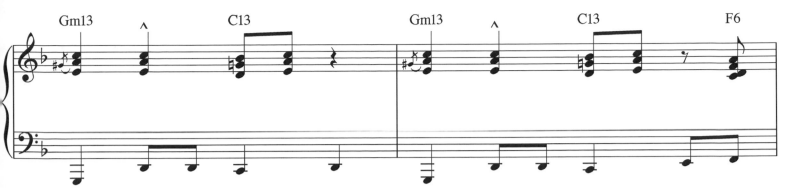

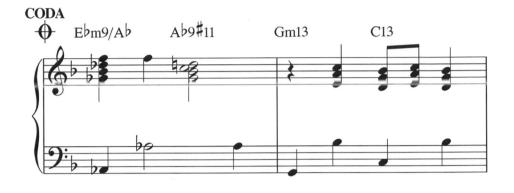

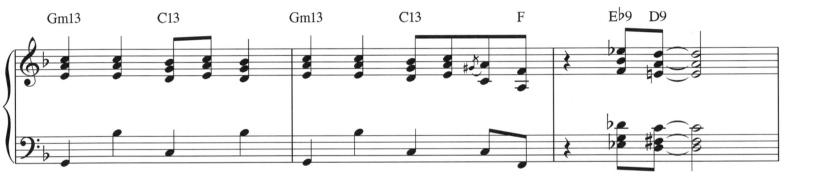

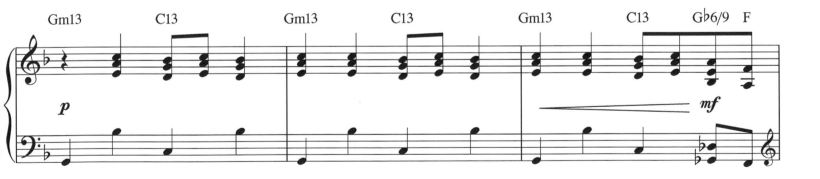

FIVE SPOT AFTER DARK

By BENNY GOLSON

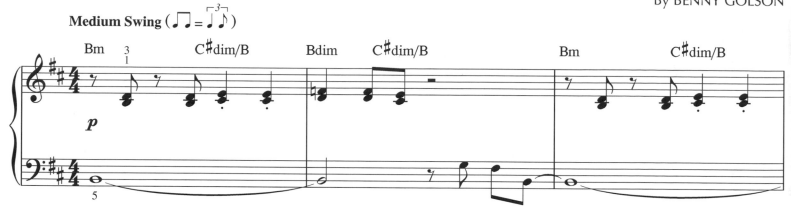

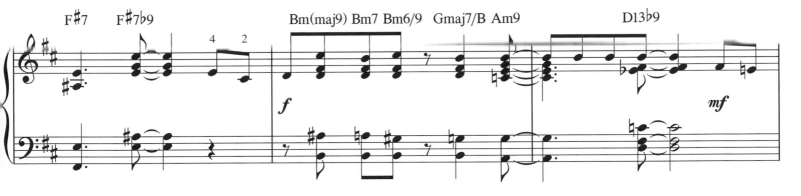

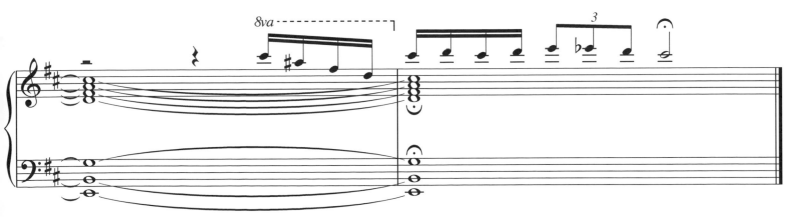

HOLY LAND

By CEDAR WALTON

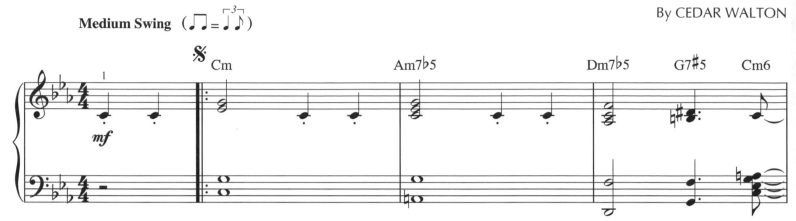

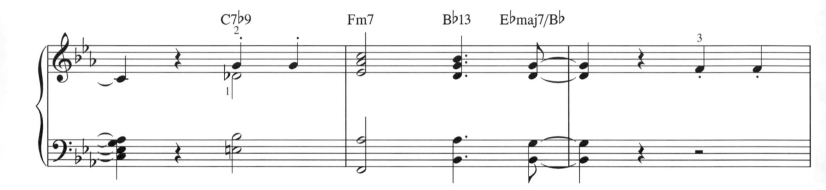

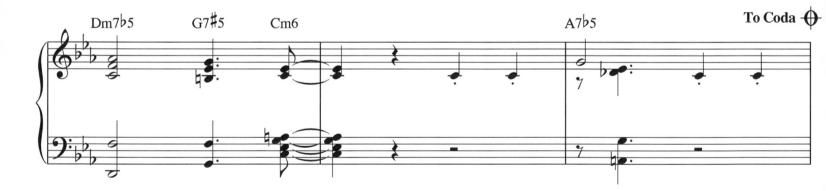

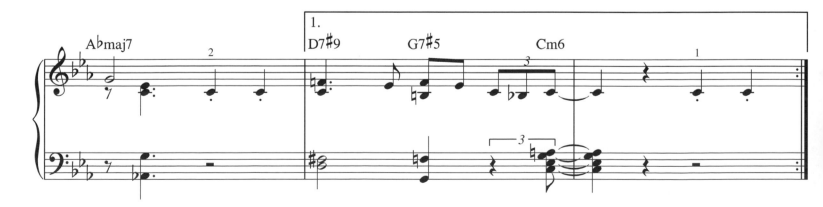

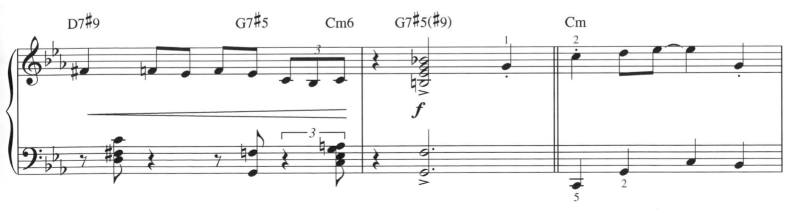

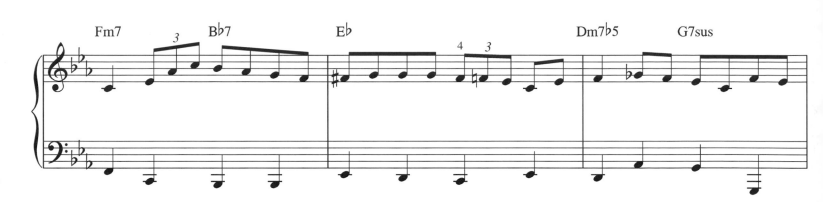

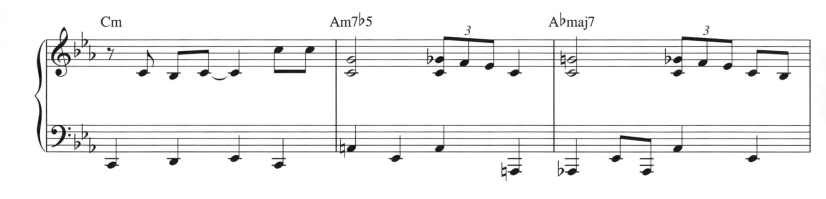

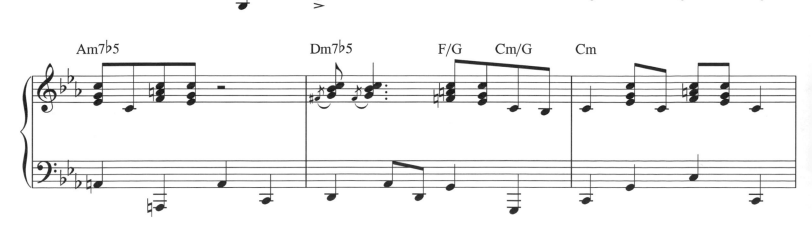

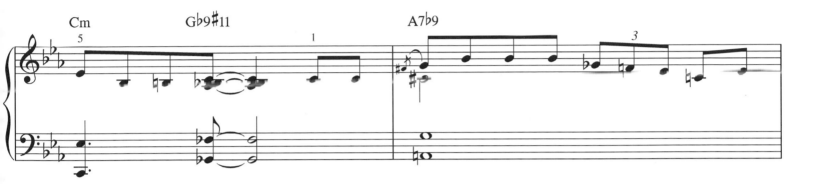

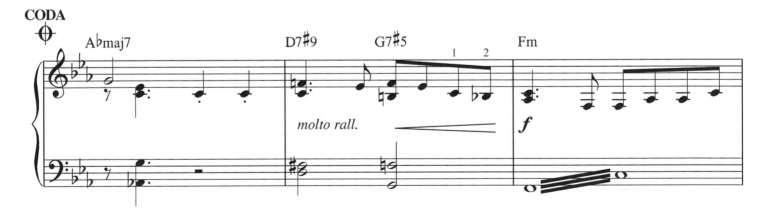

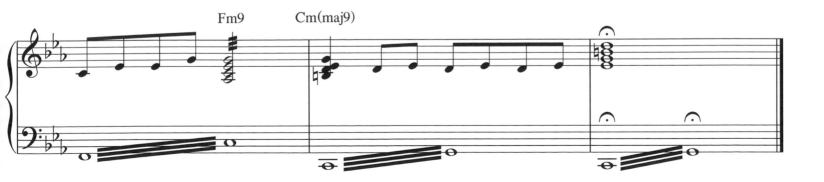

THE "IN" CROWD

Words and Music by
BILLY PAGE

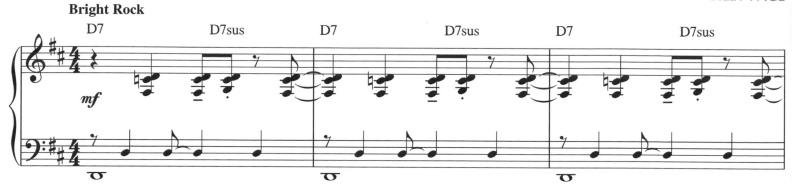

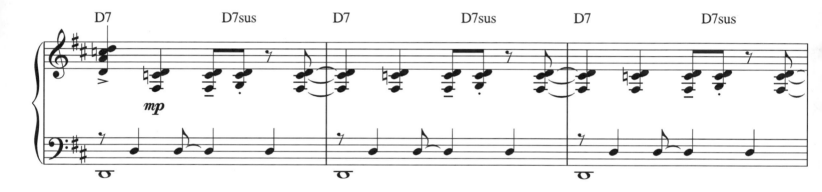

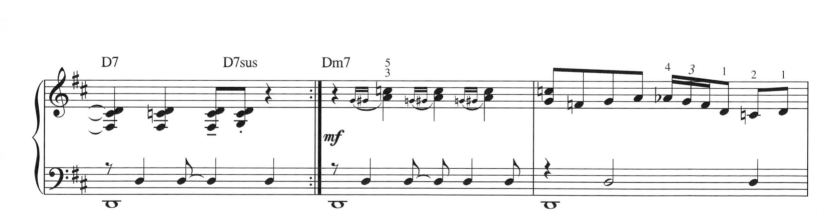

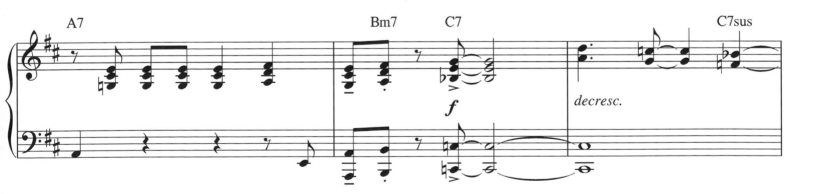

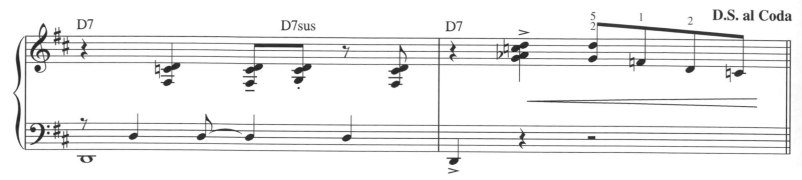

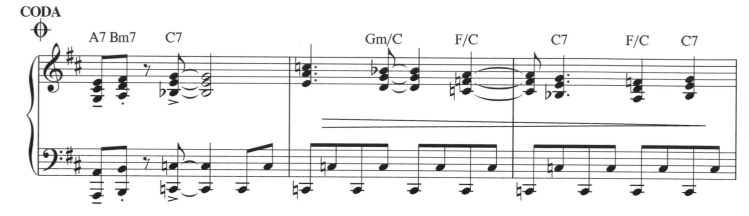

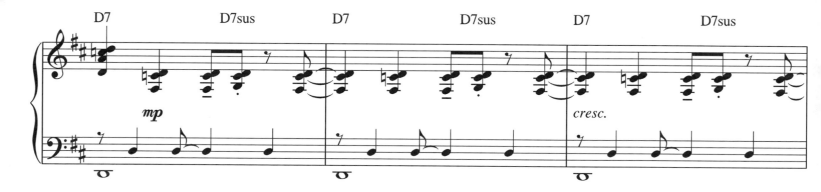

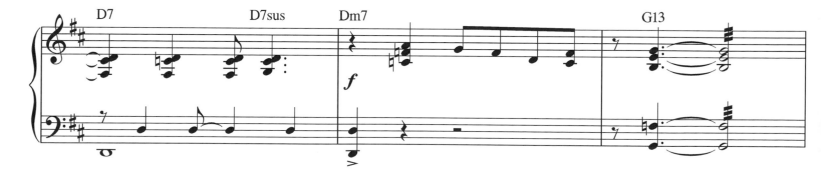

THE MIDNIGHT SPECIAL

New Words and New Music Adaptation by
HUDDIE LEDBETTER
Collected and Adapted by JOHN A. LOMAX
and ALAN LOMAX

Freely

Medium Swing (♪♪ = ♪³♪)

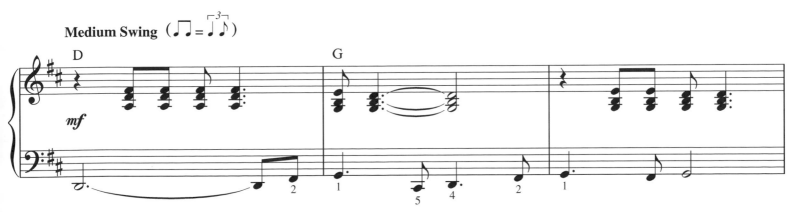

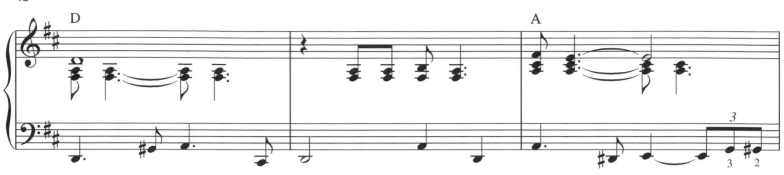

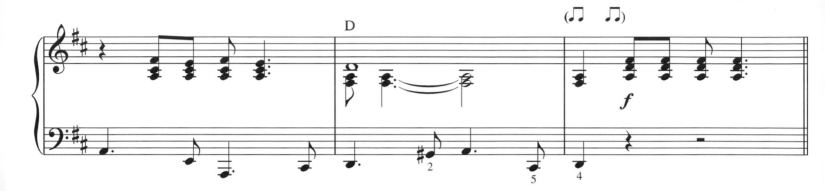

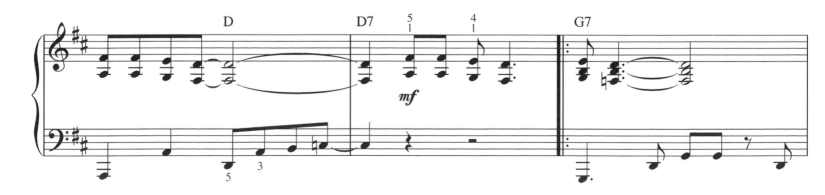

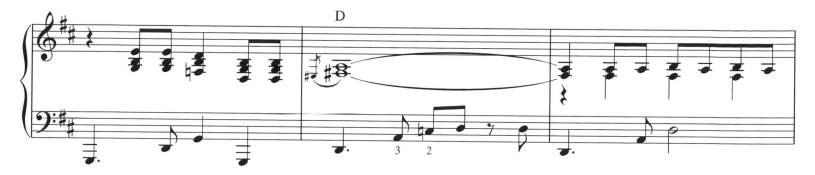

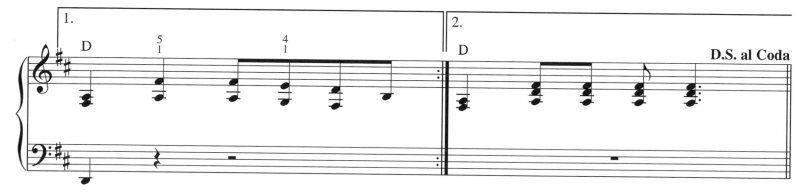

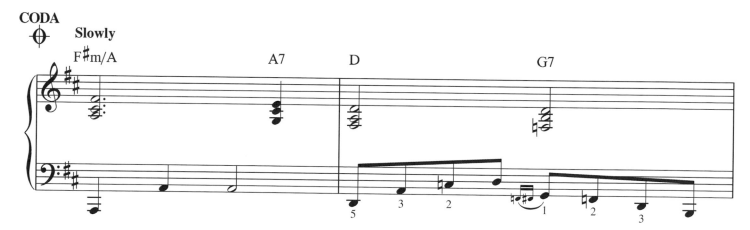

THE JODY GRIND

Words and Music by
HORACE SILVER

Funky Blues

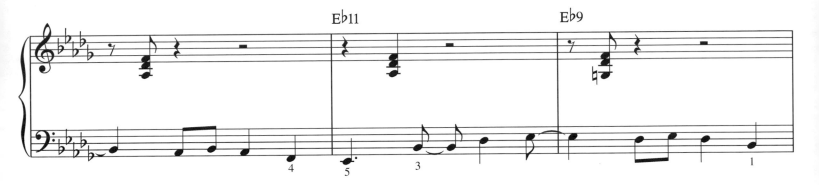

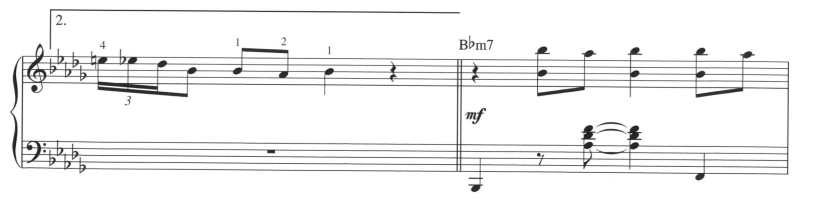

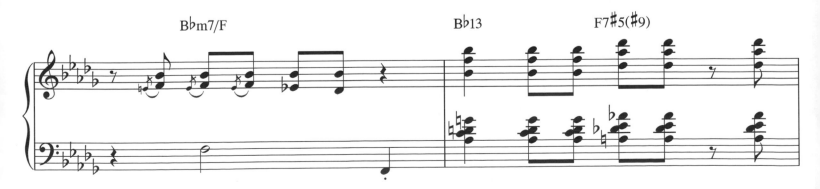

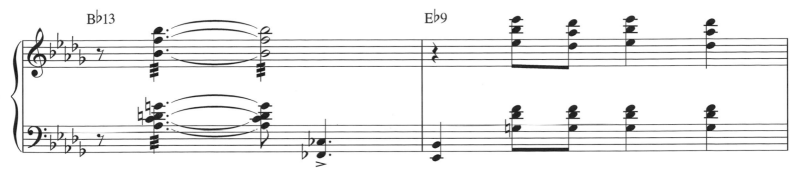

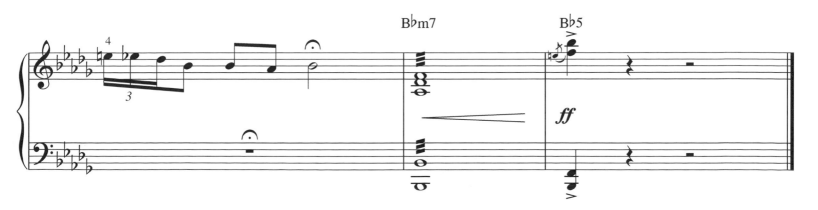

THE PREACHER

By HORACE SILVER

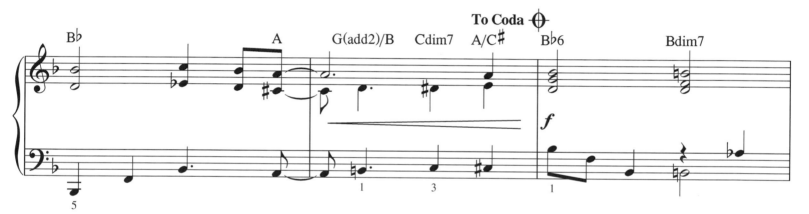

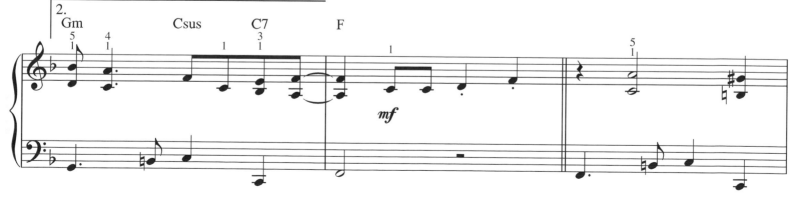

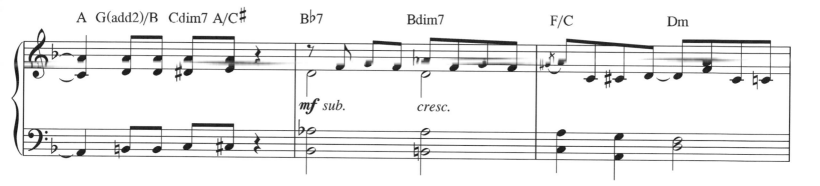

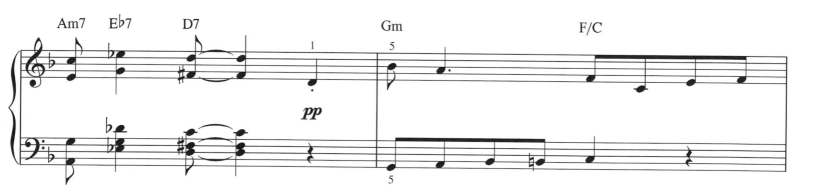

ROCK CANDY

Words and Music by
JACK McDUFF

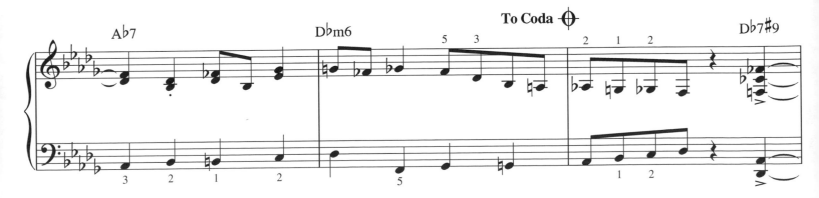

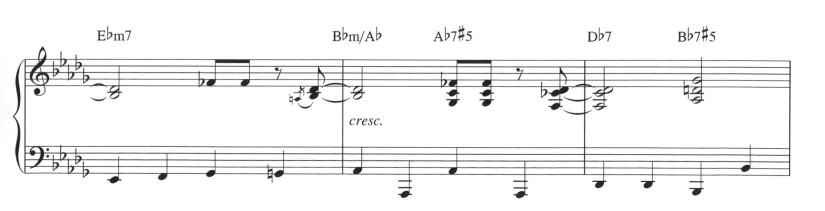

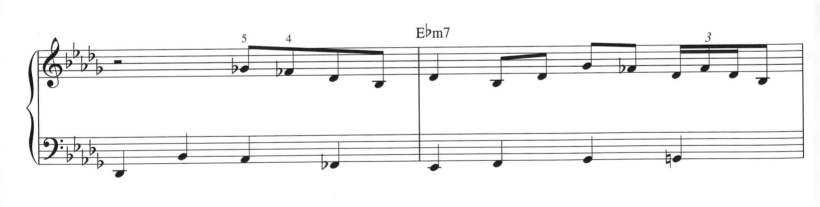

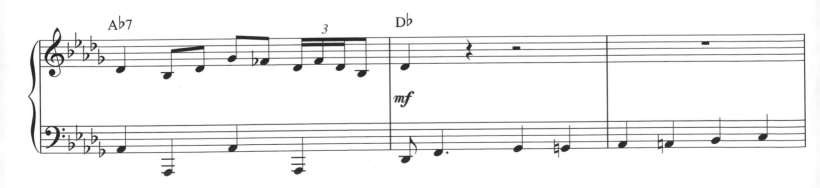

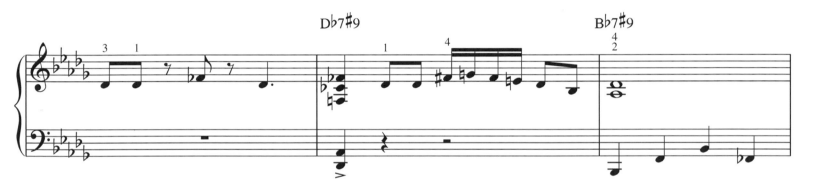

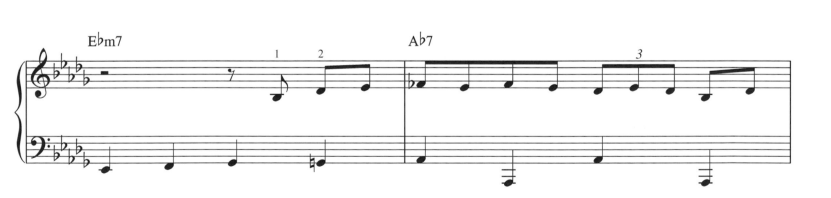

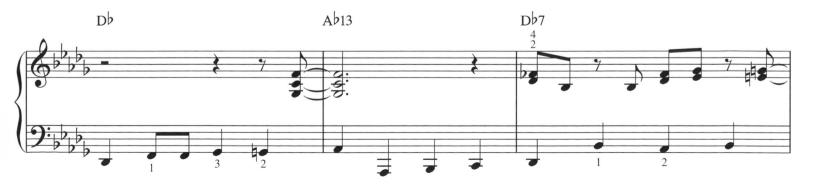

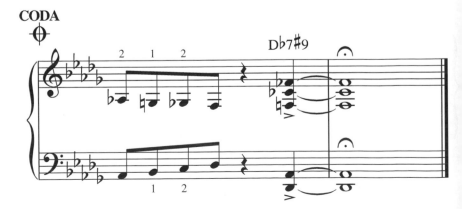

SISTER SADIE

Words and Music by
HORACE SILVER

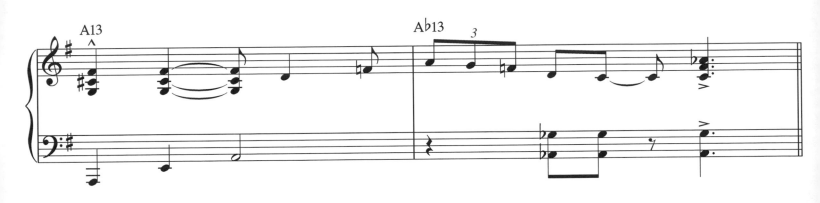

D.S. al Coda

CODA

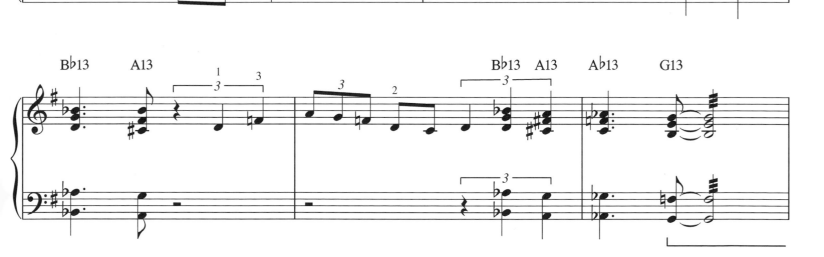

THE SERMON

By HAMPTON HAWES

Medium Swing

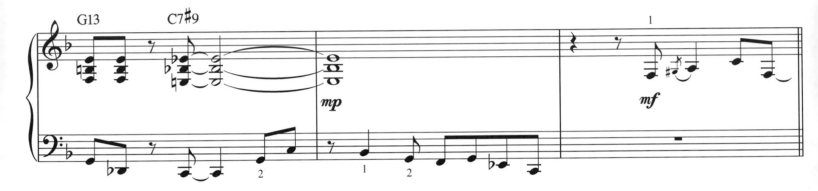

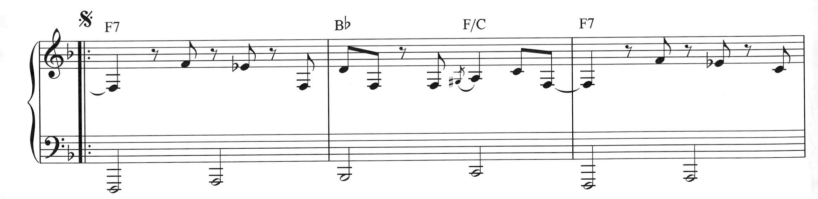

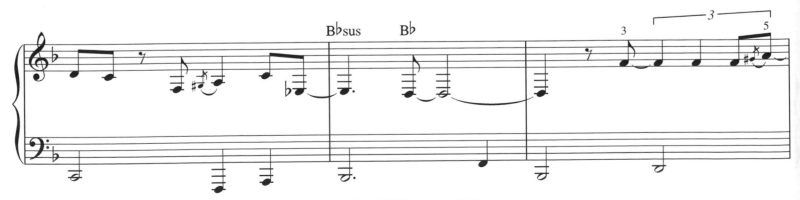

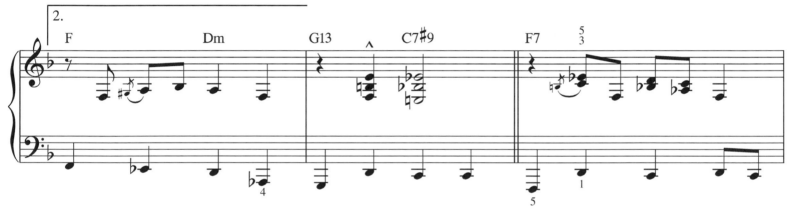

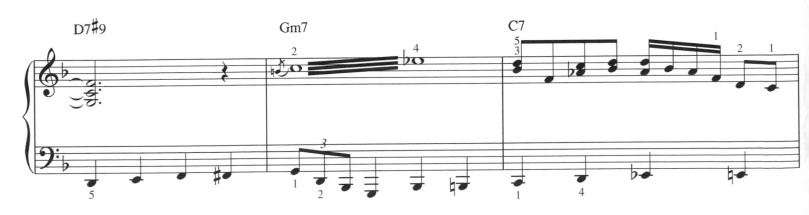

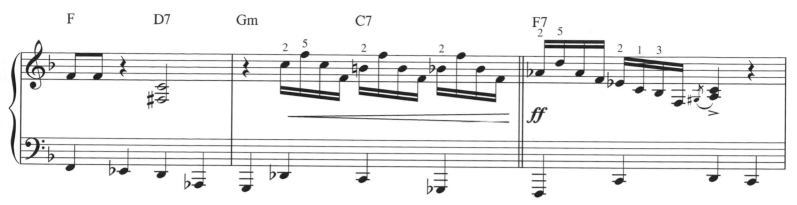

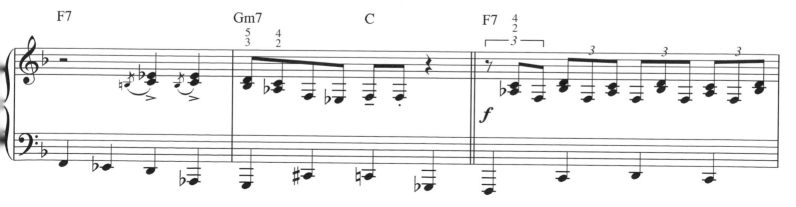

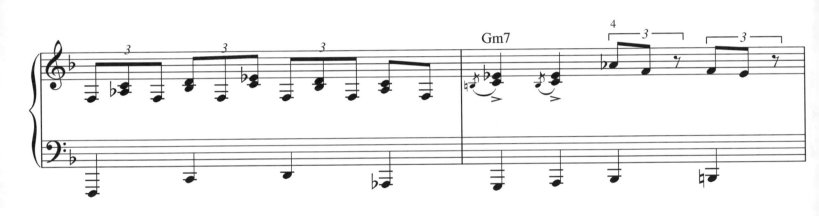

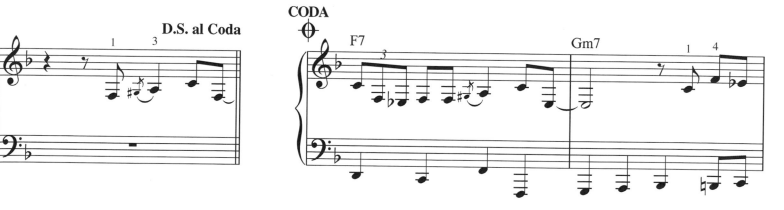

UNCHAIN MY HEART

Words and Music by BOBBY SHARP
and TEDDY POWELL

Bright Rhumba

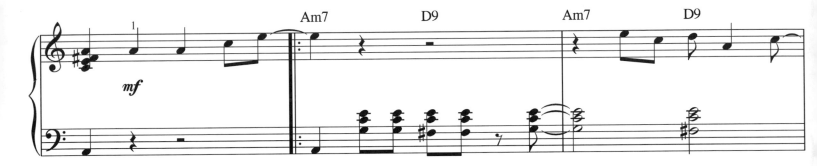

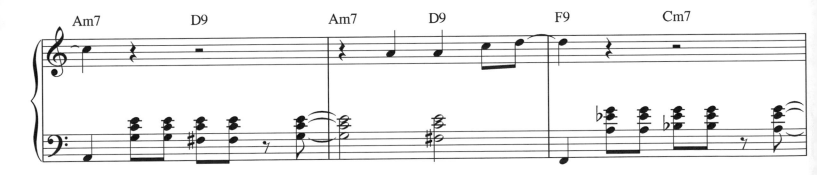

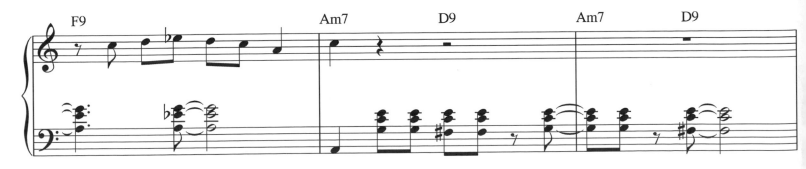

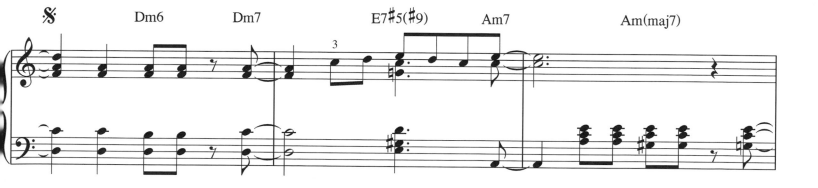

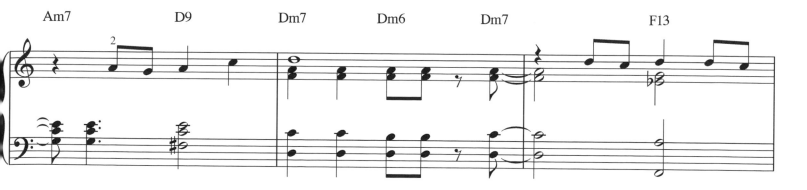

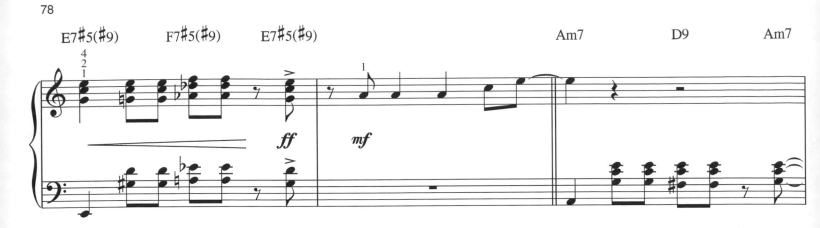

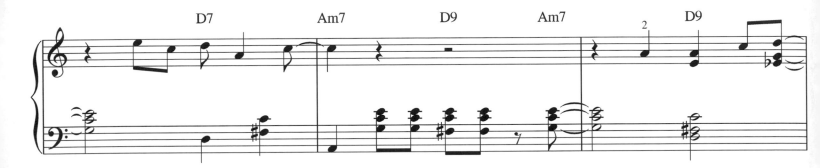

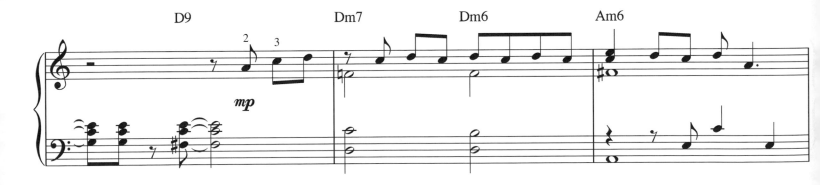

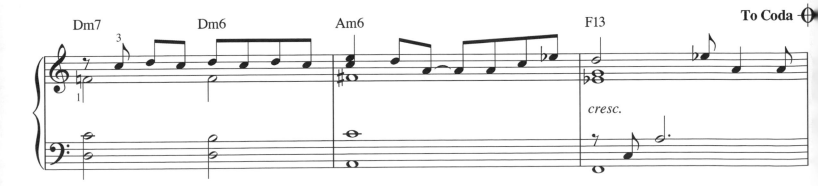

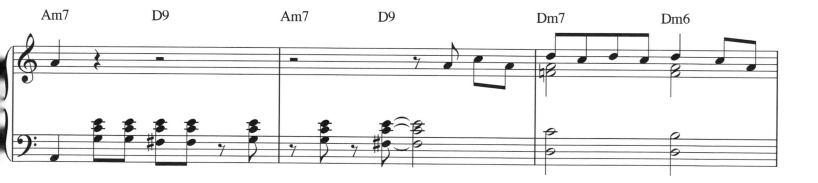

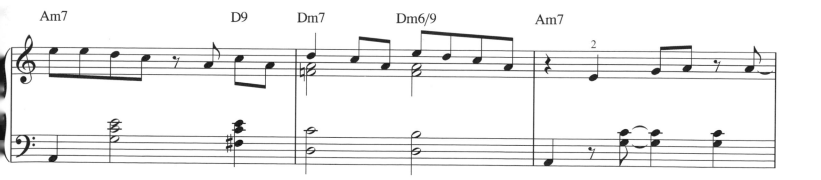

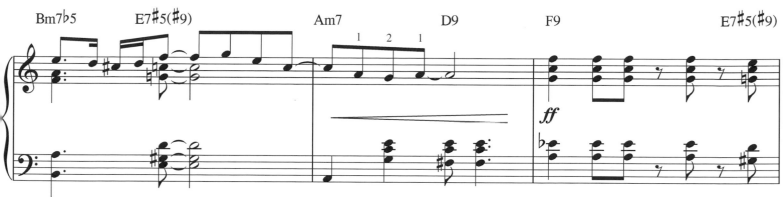

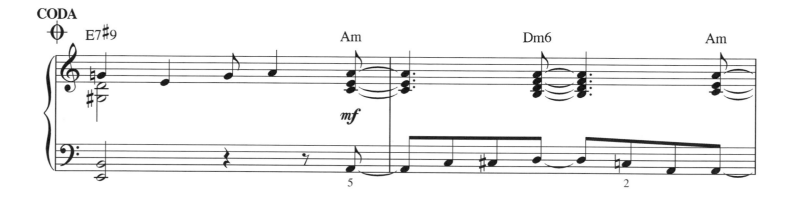

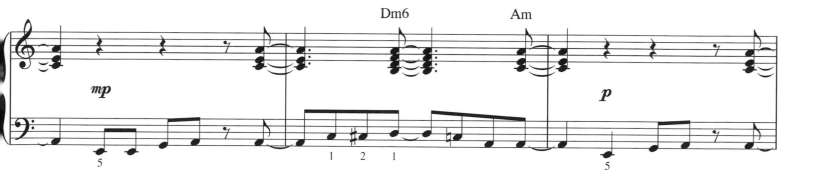

WHAT'D I SAY

Words and Music by
RAY CHARLES

Medium bounce

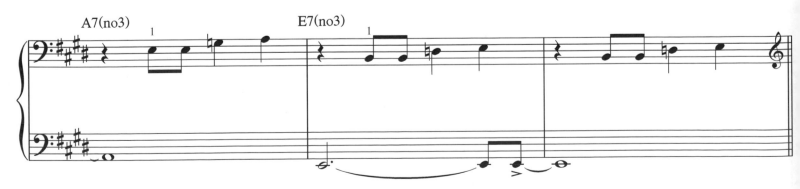

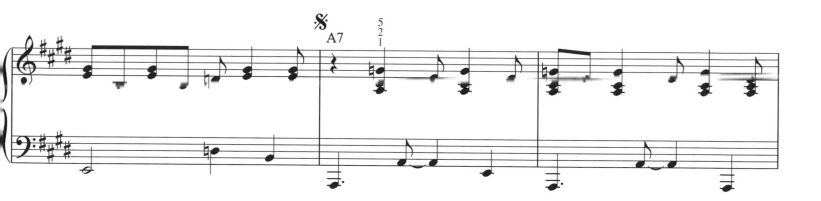

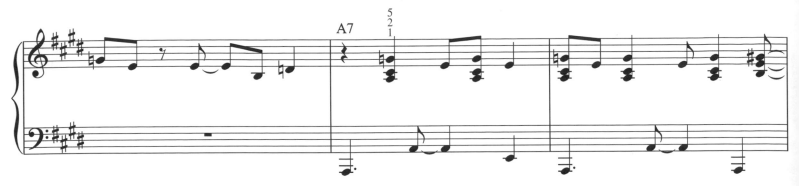

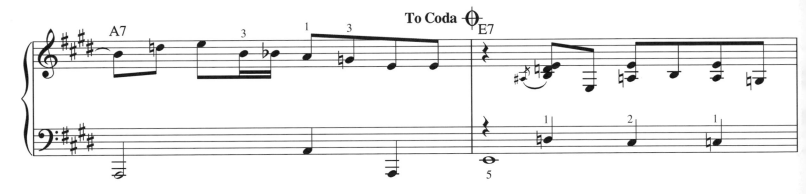

WHEN THE SUN COMES OUT

Lyric by TED KOEHLER
Music by HAROLD ARLEN

Moderately slow 12/8 feel

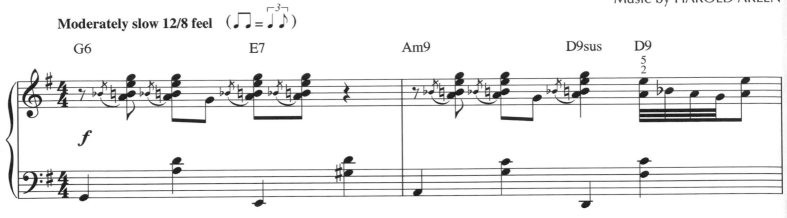

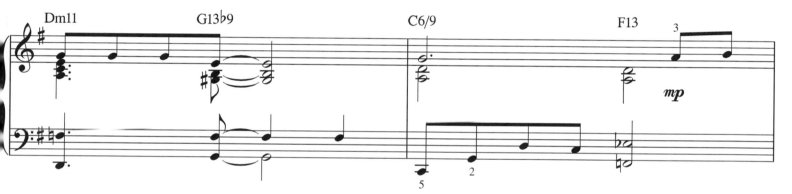

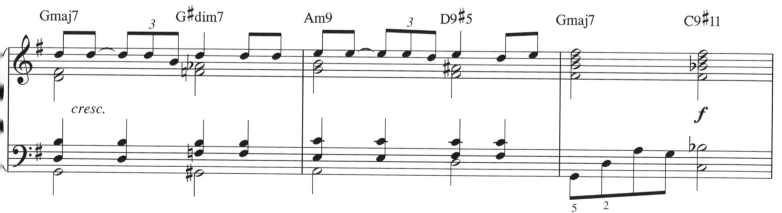

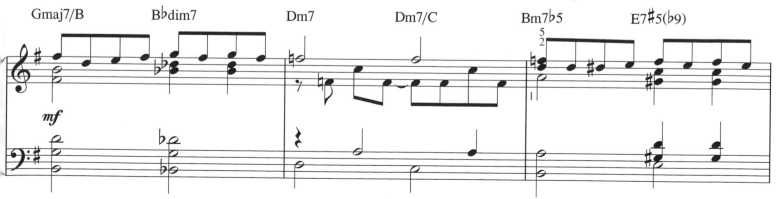

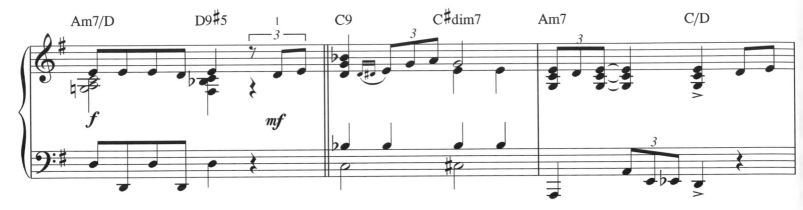

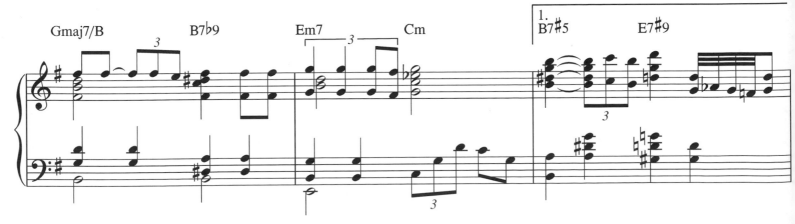

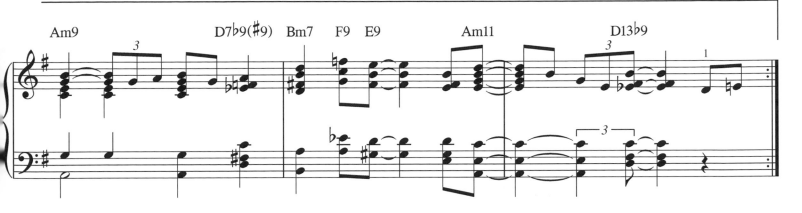

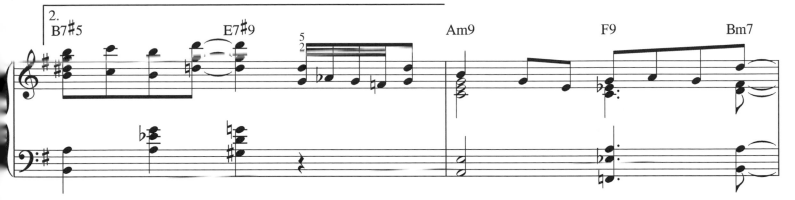

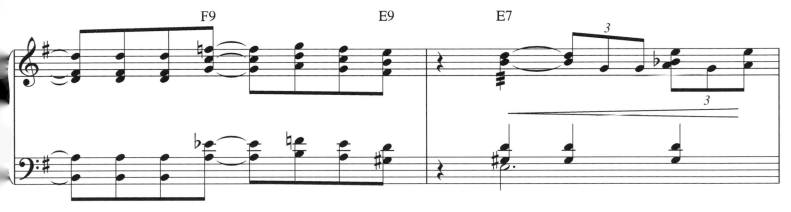

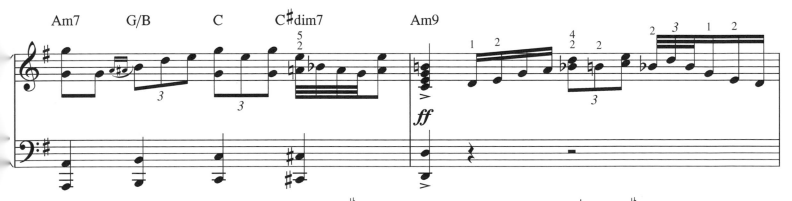

YOU ARE MY SUNSHINE

Words and Music by
JIMMIE DAVIS

Medium Shuffle

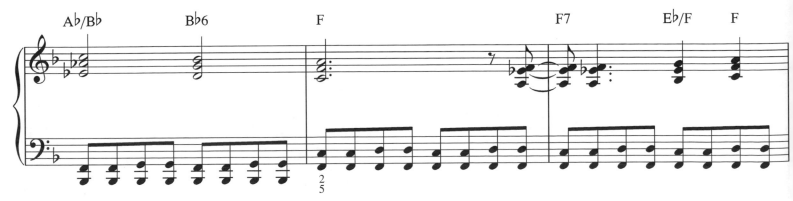

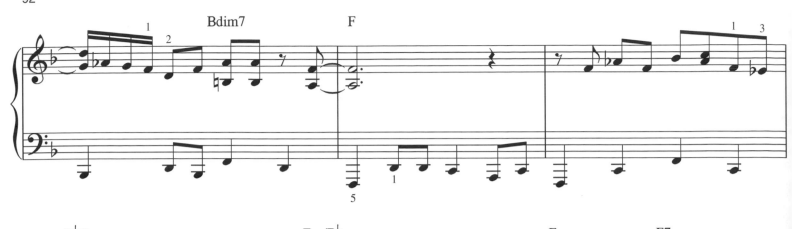

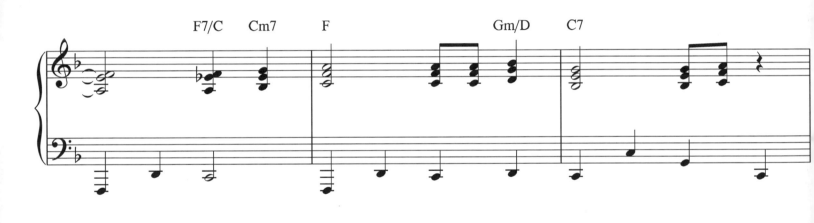

SOUL EYES

By MAL WALDRON

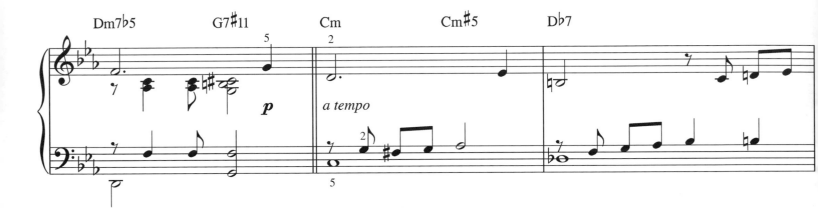

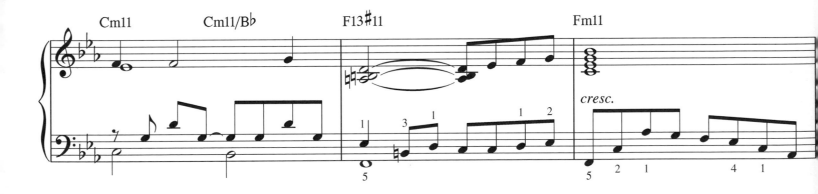

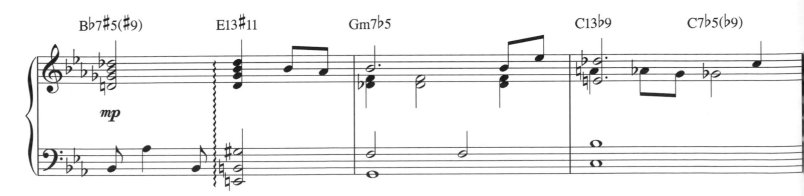

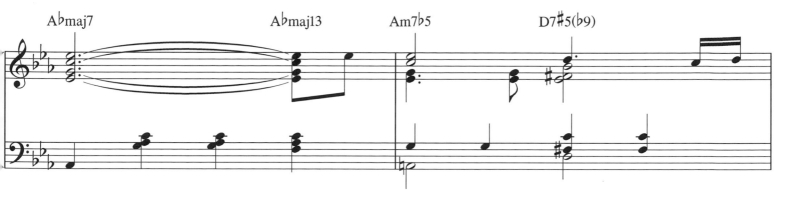

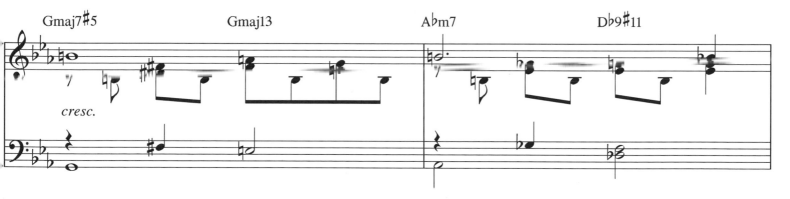

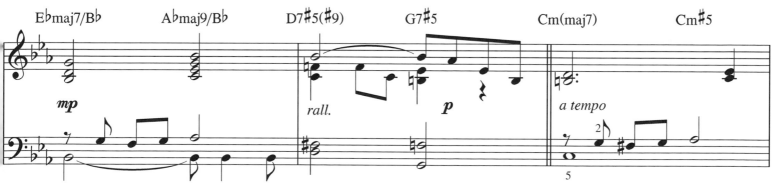

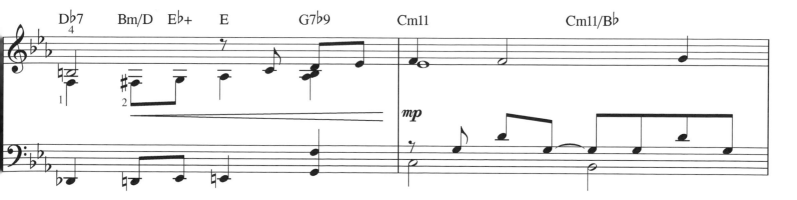

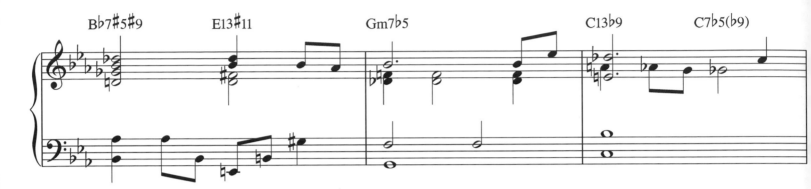